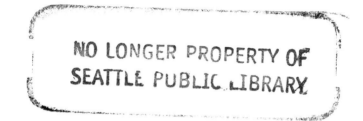

Community Helpers

Librarians

by Cari Meister

Bullfrog Books

Ideas for Parents and Teachers

Bullfrog Books let children practice reading informational text at the earliest reading levels. Repetition, familiar words, and photo labels support early readers.

Before Reading

- Discuss the cover photo. What does it tell them?
- Look at the picture glossary together. Read and discuss the words.

Read the Book

- "Walk" through the book and look at the photos. Let the child ask questions. Point out the photo labels.
- Read the book to the child, or have him or her read independently.

After Reading

- Prompt the child to think more. Ask: What is the library like in your school or town? What did you see there? What did you check out?

Bullfrog Books are published by Jump!
5357 Penn Avenue South
Minneapolis, MN 55419
www.jumplibrary.com

Library of Congress Cataloging-in-Publication Data
Meister, Cari.
  Librarians / by Cari Meister.
     pages cm. -- (Bullfrog books. Community helpers)
  Summary: "This photo-illustrated book for early readers gives examples of different things librarians do, such as ordering materials, helping patrons find information, and more"--Provided by publisher.
  Includes bibliographical references and index.
  ISBN 978-1-62031-076-2 (hardcover) -- ISBN 978-1-62496-032-1 (ebook)
  1. Librarians--Juvenile literature. 2. Libraries--Juvenile literature. I. Title.
  Z682.M45 2014
  020.92--dc23
                                        2012044151

Series Editor: Rebecca Glaser
Designer: Danny Nanos

Photo Credits: All photos from Shutterstock except: Alamy, 4, 12, 19, 21; Dreamstime, 6; iStockphoto, 8, 11, 18, 23tl; SuperStock, cover

Printed in the United States of America at Corporate Graphics in North Mankato, Minnesota.

5-2013/ P.O. 1003
10 9 8 7 6 5 4 3 2 1

Table of Contents

Librarians at Work

Ben wants to be a librarian.

What do they do?

They help people find information.

They take care of library materials.

materials

They plan story time.

8

They read a lot!

Miss May reads about new books.

She orders some.

They come in the mail.

Mrs. Hopp works at a school.
She reads to kids.
She shows them how to research.

Sun is writing a report.

She needs facts about bees.

Mrs. Gray helps her. They look in the library catalog.

Bob is looking for a job.

Mr. Rex shows him a job website.

website

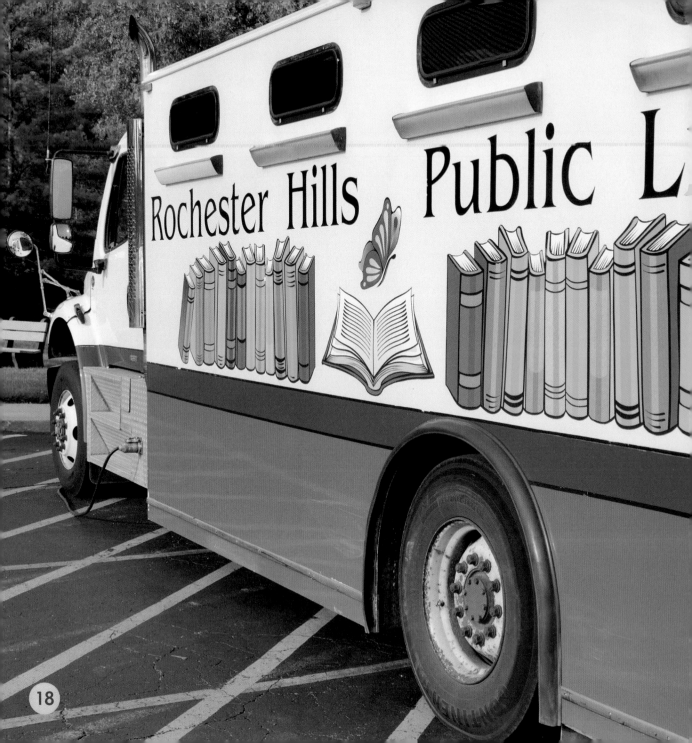

Joe cannot get to a library.

It's okay.

Miss Day drives the bookmobile.

Now he can get books.

Librarians do good work!

At the Library

shelves
Library books are put in order on shelves so people can find them.

computer
People can use library computers for research.

desk
People do work at desks.

reading area
People can sit down and read magazines or newspapers here.

Picture Glossary

bookmobile
A bus with shelves for books that a person drives to places with no library.

materials
Books, videos, magazines, or online resources that a librarian buys and maintains.

catalog
A listing of all the materials a library owns, usually stored on a website.

research
To look up facts that are known about a subject.

information
Facts and knowledge about a subject.

website
A space for information that is accessed on a computer or machine hooked up to the Internet.

Index

To Learn More

Learning more is as easy as 1, 2, 3.

1) Go to www.factsurfer.com

2) Enter "librarians" into the search box.

3) Click the "Surf" button to see a list of websites.

With factsurfer.com, finding more information is just a click away.